The Swamp Fox

written by Ross Duncan

illustrated by Robert Van Nutt

McGraw-Hill
School Division

New York   Farmington

The 1770s were a tense time in America. Relations between the thirteen colonies and Great Britain had turned sour. Many colonists felt burdened by the laws Great Britain passed on them, and some had already concluded that they would be better off if the colonies governed themselves. The British, of course, had no intention of allowing the colonies—their colonies—to declare independence and form an independent country.

War broke out in Massachusetts in 1775 and soon spread throughout the colonies. The cause of the patriots—those who supported the colonies—looked rather grim. The British were accustomed to fighting wars, and their army was large and well-trained. Most patriots, on the other hand, were not professional soldiers but ordinary farmers or laborers, and the British were, of course, better equipped to go to war. Then too, many colonists still remained loyal to Britain—these colonists, known as Loyalists or Tories, were eager to help the British.

The Americans, though, had one significant advantage: they were fighting on their own terrain. This was probably General Francis Marion's only saving grace. Before the war, Marion had been a farmer and a soldier; he had also served in the South Carolina Provincial Congress in 1775, making laws for the colony.

The British used their powerful navy and army to control Georgia and South Carolina. Marion escaped capture at the battle of Camden in 1780, when the British overwhelmingly defeated South Carolina's army. Nevertheless, that was not the end of Marion's military career. General Marion transformed a bunch of backwoodsmen into another army—one without uniforms, that received no compensation, and lived off whatever they could hunt or steal from the British. In Marion's unit, there was rarely enough gunpowder—often soldiers had only enough for two shots.

Additionally, Marion's brigade usually had fewer than 200 men, so they stood no chance against the mighty British army in open battle. At such a great disadvantage, Marion was obligated to come up with a score of new strategies and military tactics in order to turn the few advantages he had in his favor into powerful weapons.

A unit of British soldiers on horseback charged headlong into the swamp. Having pursued Francis Marion and his men all day, from the Black Mingo River to the Pee Dee River, they were finally closing in. "Onward!" shouted the British colonel, his red uniform splattered with mud.

The colonel might just as well have said, "Downward!" for, at that moment, the British horses began to sink in the loose mud. Rearing up in fright, they soon sank even deeper. Unsure of what to do, a few riders dismounted, and they, too, began to sink. Snakes, roused by the noise, slithered about. One Redcoat's mouth fell open in amazement as the log beneath his feet began to move—it was an alligator!

The British troops had obviously had enough. "Come on, lads," their colonel shouted, "let's get out of here—nobody could catch this swamp fox!"

"Swamp Fox!" General Marion repeated to himself from behind the reeds just a few hundred feet away, as he watched the hapless British struggle to reach more solid ground. Little did he know how long that nickname would follow him!

General Francis "Swamp Fox" Marion turned and
rode to his secret camp on Snow Island. Surrounded by
the swamps and rivers of South Carolina's coast, Snow
Island was the only dry land for miles around.

From a small forge, a blacksmith pulled out a long,
iron saw glowing red-hot and began to beat it with a
hammer, while other saws and a newly-made sword lay
strewn on the ground.

"How goes it?" the General called.

"Fine, sir," answered the blacksmith, "in three days
time, everyone who needs a sword should have one."

Some of Marion's men had guns, but gunpowder was
almost impossible to get. So, from their farms and
shops, Marion's men had brought saws, which the
blacksmith was busy hammering into weapons. Of
course, these swords weren't shiny and pretty like the
British ones, but their heavy blades were just as deadly
in battle.

"You'd better work faster," Marion advised the
blacksmith, "we're riding out tomorrow."

As the small army rode from camp late the following day, General Marion was worried. The American army in South Carolina had just lost a major battle at Camden. Although some men had escaped to North Carolina, most of the Americans had been killed or taken prisoner. Marion's men were now the only patriots fighting in all of South Carolina.

Near Nelson's Ferry, Marion decided to halt his soldiers and sent ahead a few scouts instead.

When the scouts returned, they reported that a huge camp of patriot prisoners was just a mile ahead—there were British guards, but not many, and all the British officers were asleep in a nearby house.

"Prisoners from Camden, no doubt," reasoned the Swamp Fox, "and the British officers must think there is nothing to fear now, but we'll show them otherwise."

At dawn, Marion's men attacked, quickly overpowering the sleepy British guards. The British officers didn't wake up until the Americans burst into their bedrooms, rifles ready. In a few minutes it was all over.

That day over 150 American prisoners were set free. Of that number, however, only three of those soldiers were willing to join Marion's army—the rest wanted to go home.

Many Southerners had become disillusioned, believing the Americans had no chance of winning the revolution and gaining independence. To be on the winning side, some South Carolina farmers were even forming a Tory, or pro-British, army.

The Swamp Fox knew all about the Tory army—his spies had watched them gathering at Tarcote and had practically taken inventory of their guns, their barrels of gunpowder, and their fine horses and saddles. The Tory army, in fact, had everything Marion and his army sorely needed.

Moving quietly, under cover of darkness, Marion's men struck at midnight—scarcely six surprised Tories had a chance to fire before the patriots closed in. Some of the Tories surrendered, while others fled into the forest.

"Shall we chase them down?" a soldier inquired.

"Let them run and hide," the Swamp Fox replied. "One day soon, they will be ready to turn patriot, and then they will be fighting on our side."

After the Tarcote raid, Marion's men were much better equipped to fight but they were still too few to face the British. How could Marion strike effectively without having his force destroyed?

Armies need food, uniforms, weapons, and ammunition. Ships full of supplies from Britain routinely docked at Charleston and Georgetown. Their contents were then carried by wagon trains to soldiers and forts across the state, so Marion sent his scouts to observe them carefully.

"A large wagon train has stopped in Wadboo Bridge for repairs," a scout raced in to report, "and another is due in Monck's Corners later today."

Twenty-five of Marion's best horsemen rode out to ambush the wagons at Wadboo Bridge. Before the guards knew it, the wagons were surrounded and, minutes later, their supplies were burning. Turning toward Monck's Corners, the raiders ambushed the second wagon train, once again taking the British guards' guns and unhitching the wagon horses. Taking whatever they could carry, the patriots destroyed the rest to keep them out of British hands.

The troops at Fort Watson were responsible for guarding the British supply lines between Camden and Charleston. Stocked with guns and powder, this fort was an especially rich prize for Marion.

Taking the prize, however, would not be easy because the fort was on a hill, entirely surrounded by a wall of logs. Meanwhile, the land around the fort had been cleared of trees, so no one could sneak up that hill without being seen. When Marion tried to get a closer inspection of the fort himself, British bullets dug into the ground near his feet.

It was clear that the Americans could not approach the fort on foot and, as they had no cannon, they couldn't blast their way in, either. Undaunted, Marion devised a clever plan and sent out groups of riders, instructing them to call at every farm and cabin and beg, buy, or borrow every ax they could find.

Then, the next day, axes began to thud in the forest beyond the fort —wood chips flew and trees crashed to the earth. Each log and wooden stake had to be cut just right.

Inside the fort, the British anxiously wondered what the patriots were up to, because they couldn't see anything at all from the hilltop—the Americans were camouflaged by the trees.

Days later, past nightfall, Marion had his men stop working and gave further orders. Teams of men now carried the logs to a spot near the fort and silently tied them together. Log by log, fastened crisscross, the tower rose—ten feet, twenty feet, thirty feet—at the top of which was a barrier with small holes for sharpshooters to shoot through.

At 4:00 A.M., the sharpshooters crouched behind the barrier, waiting for the sun to rise. The first British soldier to spot the tower through the morning mist got a terrible surprise and shouted for help. Soon the courtyard of the fort was flooded with men in bright red coats—perfect targets for the sharpshooters.

Meanwhile, the patriots on the ground took advantage of the confusion. Axes in hand, they raced across the open ground to the fort and began chopping at the log wall. When the British tried to stop them, the sharpshooters on the tower fired upon them.

When the hole they had made in the wall was large enough, Marion's brigade charged through. At that point, a white flag rose above Fort Watson—the British had surrendered!

"The British have stolen my beautiful home and turned it into a fort!" Rebecca Motte complained to Marion. "They have built a high log wall around my lawns, ruined my gardens, and killed my cattle and fowl. My children and I are forced to live in this little cabin!"

It so happened that Fort Motte also protected British supply lines, though it was stronger and much better defended than Fort Watson. Feeling bold from their last victory, some of the patriots suggested a direct attack. "We can race to the wall and hack our way through!"

The Swamp Fox shook his head and said, "Half of us would be dead before we reached the house. There is a better way, but we'll need shovels."

During the night, a deep trench was dug toward the fort. Meanwhile, General Marion met with Mrs. Motte and her eldest son to ask them whether they thought his plan would succeed.

"Indeed, General! You can even use my son's fine bow, a gift from his father," Mrs. Motte replied.

The next evening, a skilled hunter from Marion's troop crept through the trench, carrying the young man's bow and a quiver of arrows smeared with sticky pine tar.

At the end of the trench, the archer lit a small fire, held the arrow in it, then quickly took aim. The arrow, still flaming, landed high on the roof. By the time the second and third arrows hit their mark, the dry wooden shingles began to blaze.

Losing no time, the British climbed onto the roof and swiftly began to smother the flames. At that point, Marion's men raked them with gunshot until they raced down the ladders.

Seeing no other alternative, the British surrendered. Luckily, there was still plenty of time to save Mrs. Motte's house, so Marion's men entered the fort and put out the flames.

"You are a true patriot," the Swamp Fox told Mrs. Motte. "You were willing to lose your house for us. Fortunately, we can give it back to you."

By mid-1781, the winds of war were shifting. American armies had won some significant battles and France was now an ally. To reassemble as one huge army and defeat the American forces in Virginia, the British were beginning to pull their troops out of South Carolina.

While the British were still there, the Swamp Fox prepared to attack the port of Georgetown, South Carolina, where they unloaded their supplies. As Marion knew this port would be protected by large cannons, he realized that taking Georgetown would not be easy.

Or would it? As his army approached Georgetown, Marion learned that the British had already gone. Hearing that the Swamp Fox was planning to attack, they had all sailed away the night before, taking their Tory supporters with them. To the patriots in Georgetown, the Swamp Fox was a great hero—he had "freed" their city without firing a single shot!

The shooting, however, was far from over. Later in the year, the last British army in South Carolina—2,000 strong—was camped at Eutaw Springs. An American army under General Nathanael Greene had marched into South Carolina to fight them, but the British force was too large for Greene. Would the Swamp Fox help?

Of course, General Marion was only too happy to oblige. In fact, Marion's troops led the attack at Eutaw Springs. In the fierce battle, both Redcoats and colonists lost many men. When the dust settled, the British were retreating for the coast with Marion's brigade following close behind, attempting to make their retreat as difficult as possible.

After Eutaw Springs, the fighting was over for General Francis Marion. Nevertheless, there was still much to do. South Carolina had had no government for two years. With the British holed up in Charleston, the legislature began to meet and pass laws, and Senator Frances Marion took part in every session.

Although Marion was feared as a fighter, he knew when to make peace. As the American Revolution was ending, many patriots wanted him to lead attacks on their Tory neighbors to punish them for supporting the British, but Marion flatly refused.

"Enough blood has already been shed," he explained. "I shall not spill another drop of it unless Americans are attacked."

In October 1781, the British army in Virginia surrendered to General George Washington. The last British soldiers in Charleston and other Southern ports left in 1782, and a peace treaty was signed in Paris in 1783. The United States now belonged to the people who had settled there and cared about it, like Francis Marion, the Swamp Fox.